A Song and a Prayer

A Song and a Prayer

by Betty Carlson

BAKER BOOK HOUSE, Grand Rapids, Michigan

Standard Book Number: 8010-2302-5
Library of Congress Catalog Card Number: 73-115639
Copyright, 1970, by Baker Book House Company

Printed in the United States of America

To the Dahlgren sisters

(who were brought up on a farm in northern Illinois in the days of the little red schoolhouse, the new-fangled contraption, the telephone, and buckwheat pancakes, laughter and prayer for breakfast) — in appreciation of their cheerful, creative lives.

Betty Carlson
Chalet le Chesalet
Huemoz, Switzerland
2 August 1969

Portions of the material in this book appeared originally in the column, "I Love People," a weekly feature of the *Rockford Morning Star*.

Prelude

It is easy in the twentieth century to lose the reality of the Christian faith, the fact that God is near. Partly this is so because to many of those who teach us today, God is not near. The majority of clergy in our generation are occupying themselves with the unsearchable things of God, and fail to remind us of the glorious, knowable truths in Scripture which our minds can take in, and need to ponder, over and over.

When Philip said to Jesus, "Show us the Father," the answer was not a complicated discussion about a supreme being who is neither up nor down nor anyplace where a believer can readily locate him. Not at all. Christ's answer can be understood by a child: "He who has seen me has seen the Father."

If the Son of God spoke simply and plainly, should not we, His children, aim to do the same?

The following chapters attempt to declare in plain words that it is a marvelous thing to believe God. It not only cheers your own heart and gives purpose and meaning to your life, but it encourages others to trust Him too. When we delight in the Lord, He promises that we will ride upon the high places of the earth. A Christian is someone going someplace, and it is a lot higher than the moon.

Contents

Prelude

PART ONE – A SONG AND A PRAYER
1. A Song and a Prayer 13
2. Why Wait? 15
3. Round Loaves of Swedish Bread 17
4. Down the Nile 20
5. Please Send My Winter Coat 23
6. The Light Touch 25
7. The Sound of the Organ 28
8. A Hole in the Middle 31
9. What Next? 35
10. A New Song 40

PART TWO – IN GOOD COMPANY
11. In Good Company 47
12. Need All Three 50
13. See for Yourself 53
14. SMASHCRASH!! 56
15. Look Beyond 58
16. Please Forgive My Swedish 60
17. An Expensive Tree 62
18. Five or Four Miles Away 65
19. Back to Adam and Eve 68
20. Live Today 72

PART THREE – "JOY IS WISDOM"
21. "Joy Is Wisdom" 77
22. A Wise, Old Man 80
23. Pinched Faith 81
24. Better Than Nothing 85
25. A Different Angle 87
26. Are Schools Necessary? 90
27. Not Trying 92
28. Not Deep Enough 94
29. Not Always Doing 97
30. A Few Friends at the End 99

Postlude 100

PART ONE

A Song and a Prayer

1. *A Song and a Prayer*

It depends upon who told you something, and what shape they are in, whether or not the advice is worth taking. Recently a tired young mother told me that whenever her children have a sore throat or other cold symptoms, she packs them off to the doctor as fast as she can for the latest miracle drug. This is a fine system *if* you have plenty of time, good transportation, and a high credit rating.

My mother did not have it as good when she was a child. She lived on a farm near Cherry Valley, and even though there were several horses in the barn, Grandpa did not believe in hitching them up except for an emergency, church, Saturday shopping, and going to visit relatives. Furthermore, Grandma did not believe in doctors for minor ailments like diphtheria, pneumonia, or dyspepsia. She kept on hand zinc sulphate to gargle, peppermint tea to swallow, and large doses of good cheer to spread around. To be honest, my Grandmother did not believe in sickness.

That's not all. She had nothing to do with the currently popular expression, "I'm tired."

"We were not permitted to say we were tired," my mother explained. "We might have thought it while picking raspberries in the hot sun, or bringing eggs to the Chicago people who rented the cottage down by the river, but we never said it."

Part of Grandma's theory was to keep her children moving. She teased the nine children out of their icy bedrooms in the early hours of the dawn by filling the farmhouse with the fragrance of buckwheat pancakes and homemade pork sausages sizzling on the cookstove. As the chattering youngsters skipped

13

along the rag rugs into the cheerful kitchen there were heaped-up bowls of oatmeal awaiting them, and cups of hot chocolate topped with whipped cream made from the thick, fresh cream scooped from the top of the milk can. Grandma always started her morning with a song and a prayer, and her children never knew there was any other way to begin a day.

Even though Grandma did not believe in sickness, occasionally one of the children would come home from school with a cold. Grandpa, who was sitting by the stove reading the Swedish newspaper, would remove his store-bought glasses, have one of the other children hold the kerosene lamp while he peered into a red throat.

In the meantime, Grandma was cheerfully melting lard in a pan. Then she would pour in some turpentine and place the mixture on the back of the stove. The ailing child was tucked into bed and thick, woolen cloths dipped into the lard and turpentine were placed upon his chest, each one hotter than the last. "Our colds disappeared right away," my mother remembered, "but the smell of turpentine held on for days!"

I am not sure if it was the buckwheat cakes for breakfast, the fact Grandma did not believe in complaining, the turpentine and lard, or the beginning of each day with a song and a prayer, but my mother never saw a doctor until after she was married, and then only because she was having a baby. As it says in Scripture:

"A merry heart doeth good like a medicine: but a broken spirit drieth the bones" (Prov. 17:22).

2. Why Wait?

"The trouble with life is, by the time you know your way around, you don't feel like going." It sounds as if Mark Twain said that, but I'm not sure. Last week I read a biography of Gustavus Adolphus who was crowned King of Sweden at the age of seventeen. The young monarch knew where he was going even as a boy. His dignified, courteous bearing, his trust in God from early youth, was noticed by all.

At the time he was made king, Gustavus Adolphus promised his subjects that their prosperity and the maintenance of the evangelical faith would be the aim of his life — and they were. He became known around the world as "the Lion of the North and the Bulwark of the Protestant Faith." In his thirty-eighth year, before his last battle, one hour before dawn the drums beat the reveille, and the soldiers, standing to arms, listened to prayer and sang two hymns. Within a few hours the great soldier and faithful Christian perished in the fight. There is a great gulf between a man of God like Gustavus Adolphus and the anti-heroes of today and their immoral, destructive lives.

If the young king had not begun preparing himself in early boyhood, he would not have been useful to his Lord nor to the millions of people living in northern Europe. It was Abraham Lincoln who said, "I will study and get ready, and perhaps my chance will come."

It is easy to develop the mentality. Give me an opportunity and I'll get ready. Most of the malcontents in the world are in this category. They live out their whole lives waiting, whereas those who do things that are worth remembering, start in right where they are, with what they have. When the opportunity arrives, they are ready. Charles Spurgeon was a remarkable preacher before he was twenty, not because he had everything going his way, but because he was going the way of the Lord and had spiritual resources upon which to draw as deep as the deepest ocean.

Luther's good friend, Philipp Melanchthon, was lecturing in logic, mathematics and theology when he was nineteen years old. Too many of us today blame our non-productive lives on our poor circumstances, lack of opportunities, our parents, the age we live in, and the hard things that have happened to us.

Not long ago a study was made in California of the lives of one hundred successful men to see if they had been badly hindered by a poor home or undesirable childhood. The interesting result of the survey was that the majority became successful, not because of their early difficulties, but in spite of them.

Those who use their time, talent and troubles wisely and well are never losers. As an early American philosopher once said, "Did you ever hear of a man who had striven all his life faithfully and singly toward an object and in no measure obtained it?"

Success is not always the true measure of the worthwhileness of a life. The person who does his work, any work, the work which God has for him to do, with respect and care, he is the truly great man. If for some reason or other, you have been slow in finding your way around in life, it would not be too late to ask the Lord to teach you to number your remaining days, that you may apply your hearts unto wisdom.

And, Lord, teach me too. Remind us all of the exceeding greatness of Your power to us who believe.

"Now unto Him that is able to do exceeding abundantly above all that we ask or think, according to the power that worketh in us, unto Him be glory in the church by Christ Jesus throughout all ages, world without end. Amen" (Eph. 3:20, 21).

3. Round Loaves of Swedish Bread

Life down here is made up of small things. It only takes a few weeks of her time, but I know a lady in my hometown who goes to Nebraska every year. Each time I think about why she goes, and what she does, it refreshes me more than the scented face towels the Swiss Air stewardesses pass out to the passengers when they awaken you early in the morning as you draw near to your destination.

I'll call her Mrs. Bountiful, for she spends her yearly vacation at a home for handicapped children. She goes for one reason — to bake bread for the children and staff, wonderfully fragrant, round loaves of Swedish rye. Think how they must look forward to her visits and hate to see her leave!

She explained to me one day that she is not very talented, but people seemed to enjoy her homemade bread. Not very talented! I would say she is greatly gifted. One of the things the people of the world are crying to learn is how to live happily with what they have been given. True, there are many who have much more than she, but they are miserable. It takes real talent to learn how to make the most of what you have.

Mrs. Bountiful could take her modest savings and go to a resort one of these summers, but she knows she wouldn't be happy. She's a doer, and doers have to be doing. But it is wise of her to know that a change is wholesome. She always returns from her trips to Nebraska with a sense of peace about her. It is the peace of God which passes understanding, and it is given as a fragrant garland to those who do what they can in remembering the sufferings of others. It reminds me of what the Lord said about Mary of Bethany, "She hath done what she could."

Doing what you can is highly personal. There are no rules, because there are no two of us alike, happily. It wouldn't do for me to bake bread for anyone, but I keep praying that in my peculiar way I'll become more imaginative about the small ways in which I can manifest the love of God. I doubt if many of us have scratched the surface to this rewarding side of living.

A friend who lives in Switzerland loves good books. She is forever talking about books, asking others if they have read John Newton's *Letters,* or *The Life of Robert Murray McCheyne,* or whatever fascinating book she is reading. Her enthusiasm is such that often a visitor will say, "I'd like to get a copy of that book you mentioned. Where can I buy it?"

As Miss Prompt-to-Act (we shall call her) is not handy to stores, being back in the mountains a way, she would write to England, Zurich, or the U.S. and order the book for the visitor. After doing this over and over, she started ordering several books at a time, to keep on hand in case someone else might ask.

And that was the beginning of "The Book Store." It is still only a closet with five shelves, but in less than two years hundreds of excellent books, hymnals, and Bibles have gone down the mountain in the suitcases or knapsacks of those who have read everything else under the sun, but only recently have discovered the vast riches in Christian literature.

There is not much profit involved in "The Book Store," because Miss Prompt-to-Act gives away half of the books and conveniently forgets to collect in other situations. For one eventful week I was the accountant for "The Book Store," but gave up in despair. How do you balance the account when the proprietor gives away part of the merchandise? I found it interesting, though, Miss Prompt-to-Act always came out ahead. I stayed with the "system" long enough to notice there were always a few who caught on to what a good thing this was, and slipped in a little extra. Perhaps the most remarkable feature of the closet with five shelves, is, that Bibles in over a dozen languages have gone down the mountain — all because one person did what she could with what she had. Life down here is made up of small things.

4. Down the Nile

On a recent trip, some friends and I did not receive any mail when we were in Cairo. We thought it odd that not one of us received even a postcard or a forwarded gas and electric bill, but we chalked it up to the vagaries of travel and hopefully left a forwarding address.

A few days later my eye happened on a headline on a back page of the leading newspaper in Nairobi: "EGYPT FIGHTS LOSS OF MAIL." The article explained that last year two million letters and packages were reported lost or stolen from the mails in Egypt. TWO MILLION LETTERS AND PACKAGES, in case you read over that quickly and it did not sink in.

You pay a penalty for wishing to be informed. You invariably learn more than you care to know. Wouldn't I be a happier person if I still thought I was going to get some mail forwarded from Cairo?

The post office officials revealed the loss of the two million letters and packages after they had investigated 150,000 complaints. In the United States we get excited if our civic leaders don't fill up the holes in our streets after two or three phone calls; but mind you, *one hundred and fifty thousand complaints later* and the Egyptian officials finally revealed the loss to the public.

As you stand in the scorching sun on the desert, with your head bent back, staring up at the Great Pyramid at Giza (roughly fifty stories high) and built over four thousand years ago, you understand better such imperturbability. The famous pyramid contains 2,300,000 blocks of stone, with each stone weighing, about two and one-half tons. Still you can't help but wish that some of that perseverance and pluck carried over to the modern Egyptian postman. It impresses me that a nation that can raise up men to carry two million, three hundred thousand, two and one-half ton blocks and pile them into a fifty story high pyramid which has lasted over four thousand years, ought to be able to locate a few stout souls willing to tote a sack of mail around the block.

One of the more intriguing cases being investigated in the mail scandal in Cairo involves a postman who got tired of delivering his load. He was seen, late one night, standing on a bridge emptying his mail bag into the swift flowing Nile river.

Our hotel in Cairo was located on the left bank of the Nile. Now that I think about it, when we were enjoying breakfast one morning on the terrace, we *thought* we saw something floating by. One friend suggested that it was a crocodile, another, Cleopatra, while the third friend told us all to sit down and drink our mango juice; but now I know, it was our mail floating down the Nile.

Civilizations come and go. Arnold Toynbee has pointed out that nineteen of twenty-one civilizations have died from within and not because of exterior causes. It is sobering to realize how much is at stake today in the world. Egypt has no corner on the market of corruption and rottenness. The more things change, the more they stay the same.

It was Jeremiah who wrote for all time and all ears: "Thus says the Lord, Stand by the roads and look, and ask for the eternal paths, where is the good, old way; then walk in it, and you will find rest for your souls. But they said, We will not walk in it!" (Jer. 6:16, *The Amplified Bible*).

Every moral choice you and I make today will have a bearing on the sort of person we will become tomorrow. God has given us the power to choose. Even as civilizations die from within, so do men die when their souls become corrupt.

O Lord, give us the wisdom to look and ask for the good, old way, and then give us the strength to walk in it and find rest for our souls.

5. Please Send My Winter Coat

You learn a lot about people by the things they say in ordinary conversation. In the early part of the last century Francis Newman said to John Nelson Darby, "To desire to be rich is absurd; but if I were a father, I should wish to be rich enough to secure a good education for my children."

"If I had children," Darby replied, "I would as soon see them break stones on the road as do anything else, if I could only secure to them the gospel and the grace of God."

The two brilliant young men talked of many things, when suddenly Professor Newman began questioning his friend concerning his attitude toward the Bible. Darby, who was a lawyer and able to speak with clarity and conviction, made it plain that for him every word in Scripture was important. Newman, who had begun to hedge on the authority of the Word of God and who in later years held an unclear position, found this amusing.

"For instance," he said, "what in the world should we have lost if Saint Paul had never written II Timothy 4:13?" ("When you come be sure to bring the coat I left at Troas with Brother Carpus, and also the books, but especially the parchments.")

Darby answered, "I should have lost something. It was exactly that verse alone which saved me from selling my little library. No! Newman, every word, *depend upon it,* is from the Spirit and is for eternal service."

The incident interested me, because I too had been reading Paul's letter to Timothy and the same passage had meaning for me also, but in a different sense. I wondered if Paul's coat, books, and especially the parchments ever reached him. He died shortly after he wrote that. Then it caused me to think of my own feverish ways. Most of my life, it seems, I've been writing home, "Please send my winter coat. It's cold in Minnesota. Think you'll find it in the brown suitcase in the basement. If not, try the hall closet." Or, "Hate to bother you, Mother, but would you send my big dictionary? It's probably in a box under my bed. Thanks. I like it real well here in Hawaii."

Those homely words of Paul helped me to identify with him. For the Bible to be interesting, it helps if you have a warm feeling for the writers. Of course, in one sense they were special men chosen by God to write the Scriptures; but in another way, they were individuals like ourselves, a curious mixture of weaknesses and strength, dependent on our families and friends as we go through life.

Nearly all of Paul's friends turned from him toward the end of his life, and Darby too knew how lonely it can be when one has a fiery zeal for God's truth and a hatred for compromise. But Darby wasn't really alone. In the last letter he ever wrote, he echoed the words of Paul, "But the Lord stood with me and helped me."

It is worth everything, even to break stones on the road, to get to know Him, the true and living God, about whom it is written: "His name shall endure forever: his name shall be continued as long as the sun: and men shall be blessed in him: all nations shall call him blessed ... who only doest wondrous things" (Ps. 72:17, 18).

To be blessed in Him is better than riches, the "right" school, the "right" position, and all the other things the majority of the world is running after today.

6. The Light Touch

"What's so great about being young?" asked the village mailman. Some of us middle-aged muddlers were seated at the counter in the drugstore having coffee. "What do they want us to do?" he went on peevishly. "Turn over everything to them, even our right to live?"

The mailman was reading aloud and commenting on an editorial in the paper about the attitude of some young people today who discredit those over thirty. The druggist, a likeable man who has lived through the growing pains of more than one generation, laughed,

"It will balance up soon enough, Fred. Poor kids, they'll be over thirty themselves in a few years with a fresh pack of youngsters snapping at their heels!"

We decided that it is an ancient problem, growing up, and perhaps we could lessen the gap between the youth of today and those of us past thirty if more of us would remember that we are still growing, too, or should be). Thinking we've arrived is deadly. It solidifies our minds as well as our bodies. The wonder goes out of life, the delicious capacity to be surprised, delighted, and enchanted.

The arrived adult looks out the window and notices that it is snowing. "As if we haven't had enough of *that* this winter!" he groans. At the same time over at Bloom School a child is explaining to his teacher why he is covered with snow. "The snow was very, very deep," his eyes are dancing, "and I said to myself, 'How nice it looks,' and so I started to roll and roll and...."

It is not for nothing that one of the under thirty critics said,

25

"Old people [meaning any of us over thirty, of course] are always talking about life after death, but what about life before death?" Yes, a good question, and here are some more. Why do older people forget how wonderful it is to be alive? Why do we stop learning? Why do we not marvel more often to one another?

A prominent man who lived creatively into his eighties had this answer, "The trouble is that we don't get interested in the commonplace things — and it is the commonplace things that go to make up the universe." Many of the great poets and artists would agree. Life only becomes truly alive when we learn to respect the little things that hardly anyone sees and hears but when they are loved and cared for sometimes become unexpectedly marvelous and beyond measuring.

It was the poet, Rilke, who said that we should not completely forget "the expectant, glad-timid Christmas children" we were once, "upon whom great surprises descend like angels from within and without...."

In other words, too many of us, too much of the time, lose the light touch. Instead we bear down on life with a heavy hand. "Shut that door I'm freezing!" the mother yells at her teen-age daughter who has rushed into the yard to smell the lilac bush bursting with blooms. The father to his son, "No, it's the third time you've asked me to take you fishing. The answer is NO! I don't believe you appreciate what a busy man your father is, Robert." "You're going to let them have motor bikes?" the grandfather says sharply to the mother of four sons, forgetting completely the passion of his youth, a brown and white pony which he raced through his town raising dust and comments.

The only reason I am prodding you and me to dare to put some excitement and joy into living, to look around appreciatively and be thankful, to be more imaginatively alive is because that is what the Lord has in mind for us. It is the song of conversion. Believe in me, follow my way, Christ says, and I will make all things new. It is one of the beautiful melodies in the Bible. His mercy, his compassions are new every morning.

It is in this spirit of going on with Christ that He gives us the ability to overcome in spite of limitations, impossible hurdles, the crushing things that can and do happen to men and that would make us jaded, weary and broken in spirit. Those who are indwelt with Christ learn to get satisfaction from struggle as the hard things are turned into achievement.

Today might be a good day to try the light touch rather than the heavy hand and get back into communication with the young. A good starting point is to read Ephesians 3, beginning at verse 14:

"When I think of the greatness of this great plan* I fall on my knees before God the Father (from whom all fatherhood, earthly or heavenly, derives its name), and I pray that out of the glorious richness of his resources he will enable you to know the strength of the Spirit's inner reinforcement — that Christ may actually live in your hearts by your faith. And I pray that you, firmly fixed in love yourselves, may be able to grasp (with all Christians) how wide and deep and long and high is the love of Christ — and to know for yourselves that love so far beyond our comprehension. May you be filled through all your being with God himself!

"Now to him who by his power within us is able to do far more than we ever dare to ask or imagine — to him be glory in the Church through Jesus Christ for ever and ever, Amen!" (*The New Testament in Modern English*: Phillips. Used with permission.)

---

*Paul explains the "great plan" in verses 1-13, but briefly it is that the Gentiles are equal heirs with God's chosen people in God's timeless purpose centered in Christ.

7. *The Sound of the Organ*

True things are not always said by the upright, respected people in your town and mine. Sometimes it takes a derelict to set up a longing in our hearts.

"Waiting, watching the street and the gate from the dark study window, Hightower hears the distant music when it first begins. He does not know that he expects it, that on each Wednesday and Sunday night, sitting in the dark window, he waits for it to begin."

Hightower is a character in one of William Faulkner's explosive and beautifully written novels. He is no one's neighbor. You or I walking down one of our streets would never point and say, "Hightower lives in the second house from the corner." He is like no one we have ever met, yet he is completely plausible. After a few pages you feel his tension, his cruel sorrow, his confusion; you almost think you understand why he is the way he is. You never really like him, though, and after you walk in his shoes a few paces, eagerly you reach for your own shoes, your own burdens.

Hightower was told early one morning, a Sunday morning, that his wife, who was visiting in another city, had jumped or fallen from a hotel window and that there had been a man in the room with her. Hightower refused to give the reporters, who were waiting for him on his porch, a statement; he brushed past them and went to his church to conduct his usual service. A photographer tried to take his picture, but he pushed him aside and made straight for his pulpit.

It was the last time Hightower stood in a pulpit. His congregation finally drove him away from the church, tactfully, of course. They realized *he* wasn't to blame, but it didn't seem proper, you know, a minister having a wife who ... aaah, well, *you* know.... Then to the consternation of all, Hightower bought a little house in the shadow of his church, and there lived out his tormented life.

He never went to church again, neither to preach nor to worship. He scarcely prayed; but the church bells, the sound of the organ on a warm summer night when all the windows in the little church were open, the old familiar hymns, he knew almost to the second when he should begin to hear them. He could see in his mind the organist (she had been dead almost twenty years) rise and enter the organ loft. It was time for the Sunday evening service. To Hightower it always seemed that in that hour man approached nearest of all to God. Then alone, of all the other church meetings and gatherings, came something of the peace and joy which is the promise and the end of the church. There his heart could be quiet for a little while beneath the cool, soft blowing of faith and hope, the week and its whatever disasters finished, and the new week and its troubles and pain not yet born.

I too miss the Sunday evening service. As a child I can remember going with my parents to the friendly parish hall where the service was held. Like Hightower, I can hear some of the hymns we sang, not the formal ones of the morning worship, but joyous, simple ones, like "Saviour, Like a Shepherd Lead Us," and "I Need Thee, Every Hour I Need Thee," and "On Christ the Solid Rock I Stand," and best of all, "When We All Get to Heaven, What a Day of Rejoicing that Will Be." And the singing would be followed by an informal, cheerful message of hope and better days ahead, far ahead, sometimes.

What losers we are for having given up our Sunday evening services. Hearts never change. Maybe none of our lives are as bankrupt as Hightower's broken life, but each of us has his faggot of loneliness, confusion and frustration which the tinsel of TV can never give hope for the following week. It was King David of Israel who wrote, "I was glad when they said unto me, Let us go into the house of the Lord" (Ps. 122:1). David knew the heaviness of a heart burdened with sin, but he always found his way back to God through penitence and worship.

8. A Hole in the Middle

Spring came slowly, almost grudgingly that year in northern Italy. To the young American opera singer things seemed out of joint. She picked up the phone one dreary day in March and said to a friend,

"Let's go to Switzerland for Easter. I want to get out of this gloomy place. We could visit that family they mentioned at the class the other night." Jane laughed, "It's possible they may even be missionaries, perish the thought, but I simply have to get away for a few days."

The singer turned from the phone, satisfied to have settled that matter, but still uncomfortably aware of the emptiness she had known for years. But why? On the surface she had everything the world counts important, prominent family background, a successful career, friends, excellent health, a wide range of talents and interests besides her music, and much more. As long as she was singing or in the company of friends, all was well; but it was the solitary moments in hotels, on planes and trains, when she walked in the park in Milan, that the longing for something real, something that she didn't have, gripped her. It would steal in like fog, and then, as noiselessly, be gone.

"It is difficult to explain even today," Jane once said. "You know the British sculptor, Henry Moore, whose figures all have a hole in the center; well, that's the way I felt — empty inside."

Switzerland was as dreary as Italy that Easter weekend, and much colder, but the small Swiss village in the Alps shrouded in a gray fog was nevertheless a peaceful haven. Her host and hostess, Mr. and Mrs. Francis A. Schaeffer, were interesting and charming. Like most of the opera singer's friends, they knew a great deal about music and art, but in three ways they were startlingly different. For one thing, they really believed the Bible. And more surprising, they lived by it as if they thought God was as interested in them as the people of the Old and New Testaments. And, they were happy! She noticed this, especially. In the nervous, competitive, scheming theatrical world, it is rare to find a genuinely happy person. By nature Jane had a cheerful outlook, a rollicking, spirited disposition, but the tension in the theater, the bickering among the opera singers, the high pitched temperament of directors, maestros and stage hands did not allow for much happiness.

Sunday evening found Jane seated by the fireplace in the living room of Chalet les Melezes talking to Mr. Schaeffer. She was beginning to relax and enjoy herself, thinking that *for missionaries* they had surprisingly good taste and broad interests. In the conversation, Mr. Schaeffer asked casually, "Jane, are you a Christian?"

Never in her life had anyone asked her such a question. She blurted out something about, "I think I am," and changed the subject. Shortly after, several others came into the room, and a discussion about the reliability of the Bible got underway. After a "polite" interval, Jane excused herself and went to her room.

To sleep? No. For one reason, it was cold. The hot water bottle Mrs. Schaeffer had given her did not remove the mountain chill in the airy, four-bed bedroom; but more important, she was disturbed by Mr. Schaeffer's question, and the more bothered she became, the more irritated she was with herself for letting one impertinent question disturb her.

Finally the fog and gray of Sunday morning arrived, and with the others, Jane attended the church service conducted by Mr. Schaeffer in the living room. Strangely enough, as he prayed, her irritation was suddenly gone.

After the service Mrs. Schaeffer served a lovely Easter dinner. Again Jane could not help but notice and respond to the warmth and friendliness of this family. During a lull in the table conversation, the opera singer became aware of the ticking of the antique clock in the corner of the room, and "Suddenly I was stabbed with the realization that I could not endure living much longer without knowing *why* I felt so empty when I had everything you're supposed to want in life," she explained later.

Monday came, the day Jane and her friend had planned to leave on the 5 o'clock bus. In the afternoon, Mr. Schaeffer invited Jane to go for a walk above the chalet. She was right about the family. They were missionaries, all right, to the core; but the work they were doing, and they, themselves, were not in keeping with her idea of missionaries. Fitting the pieces together, she had discovered that many people visited the Schaeffers, especially university students and those interested in the intellectual and cultural problems of the day.

On Sunday evening there had been an interesting and particularly clear discussion of the saying of Jesus, "Except a man be born again, he cannot see the kingdom of God." This time Jane remained for the study and she listened intently. She continued to marvel that this family took the Bible seriously, and so quite naturally as she and Mr. Schaeffer started up a steep path, they were speaking about the Bible. He spoke with conviction about the trustworthiness of Scripture. This was new to Jane who had learned from her youth that the Bible was full of myths and errors, and there was a great gulf between God and man.

Then Mr. Schaeffer spoke of the unity which existed between the Old and New Testament. This interested Jane tremendously. Never had it entered her mind that there were scholars today who took the Old Testament and considered it history.

They arrived at a point just above the village, when Mr. Schaeffer glanced at his watch, "We must turn back or you'll miss the bus."

"You were saying...."

The bus was no longer important to Jane.

Mr. Schaeffer continued to tell the singer about Abraham, his call to sacrifice Isaac, and of God's providing a sacrifice in the place of Isaac. He then went on to point out how two thousand years later, on the same mountain where God had provided a substitute sacrifice, the Lord Jesus Christ had been offered up.

His words were as lightning to the one walking beside him, for she had begun to piece together the awesome truth that the God revealed in the Bible is the God of all history. With this came the realization that, by the spirit of the Living Lord, she had been led to this place, at this moment, to have her doubts dispelled.

While they were speaking, the fog, which had been hanging heavily over the mountains and village all weekend, suddenly broke apart. A shaft of light poured down, and for the first time, Jane saw the majestic peaks.

"Amazing!" she murmured, but the warmth and the light of the love of God which was moving into the empty place deep within her, was infinitely more glorious than the panoramic view before her.

The bus had long since left when the two retraced their steps down the mountain. The musician had a strenuous session ahead with her manager to explain why she stayed away an extra day; but for the first time in years the singer's mind was not centered on opera.

A few weeks after Jane returned to Italy, she wrote a letter to Switzerland:

"I know that it was part of the plan that I missed the bus on Monday. How wonderful to have my blinded eyes opened! Thank you, dear Mr. and Mrs. Schaeffer, for quietly and simply showing me the pathway I have been searching for so long."

9. What Next?

After her conversion, Jane Stuart Smith continued her opera career, but now her Bible and the encouraging letters from her new friends became her companions on the lonely tours. Several different evenings, following her return from the Swiss Alps, she gathered her opera associates in her room or the hotel lobby and told them of her recent experience. A few showed interest, one or two asked questions, but the majority couldn't care less.

"This was a shock," Jane recalls. "I thought other people would be as excited as I was to learn that God is real, and that the cross of Christ is not just a piece of theater, but flaming evidence of how much God cares for us."

Almost immediately when Jane returned to Italy, she enrolled in several correspondence courses with a view of gaining a clearer understanding of the Bible. Often she worked on the studies in her dressing room in the tense moments before going on stage. Besides teaching her, she welcomed the quiet strength the Word of God gave to her in these moments of great tension.

But the sharp, two-edged words of Scripture did something else which the opera star had not counted on. They gave her an uneasy feeling that she was being moved toward a decision, but she brushed away the idea as preposterous. God had given her her voice, her acting ability, the hard, long years of training, the many successes she was now enjoying — surely He would not take her out of opera. It was her life — the thing she knew best and in which she was at her best.

Jane continued to receive the lead roles in the operas she

sang, and her performances always won the highest praise. Her manager, her maestro and other supporters were delighted with her success. They could see their rising young star becoming one of the great Wagnerian dramatic sopranos of the day. That Miss Smith should give up opera was unthinkable.

"It happened much sooner than I ever dreamed it would," Jane explained. "It was while I was singing Brunnhilde in *Die Walkure* in Naples that I knew with certainty this was my last opera. I can't tell you how I knew it. It didn't make sense to me, but the certain final feeling was there."

Those who heard the performance that night said it was an unforgettable experience. At the close of the last act, the audience stood and applauded, shouted and stamped their feet. They were trying to tell the star they thought she was great.

"I didn't tell a soul it was my last performance," Jane painfully remembered. "In a sense I didn't really believe it myself, but I couldn't shake that 'feeling.'"

Confirmation came in an unexpected way. Passing through New York on the way to her home in Virginia, she stopped to visit her sister and family. The morning after her arrival the children came tumbling into the guest room to see Aunt Jane. They loved to hear about her glamorous life, the different countries she had visited, the important people she knew. But this time she spoke of something completely foreign to them. She told them about the tabernacle in the Old Testament, a subject which was beginning to be a favorite with her. They listened intently as Jane described how God told Moses to tell the children of Israel to bring gold and silver and brass for the tabernacle, and blue and purple and scarlet and fine linen for His sanctuary where He might dwell among them. It was not difficult for the opera singer to tell a vivid story.

Finally one of the children said, "You mean all that's in the Bible?"

Another niece, who was also spellbound, said thoughtfully, "You know, Jane, after you've had your opera career, you could become a missionary!"

That remark went straight to the heart of the singer.

"It was exactly what I had in mind to do," Jane explained. "Give God the leftovers. I was the one who had chosen opera for my life. This was not God's choice for my life, even though for quite a while after my conversion I thought I could serve Him in that role; but I was rapidly seeing that I had little time for God as my career advanced."

The next few weeks were torture. The peace and joy Jane had found in Switzerland vanished. She was more miserable than she had ever been in her life. The new convert was incapable of a decision.

"I had no words to explain why I was leaving the theater," she said. "It might have helped if I had some plan in mind, if I could have said, 'God's calling me to be a missionary in India.' But I had no specific call. All I knew was that opera was beginning to pull me in a different direction from the way of Christ which *I* had chosen, and I had been given an inner conviction that for me to continue to sing opera would be against the counsel of God."

Jane particularly dreaded telling her Mother, her maestro, and her manager, these three who had sacrificed so much to put her where she was and were so thrilled at what she had accomplished as a young singer, and were dedicated to her future. How could they be expected to understand her decision to give it all up, when she scarcely understood herself?

When Jane prepared to go back to Europe after her visit in the U.S.A., she still could not find the words to tell her parents that she had sung her last opera. Her Father, a very sensitive and understanding man, knew his daughter was struggling with something larger than her life, but he did not know specifically what it was. When he put her on the train for New York, the last thing he said to her, "Don't give up your music."

Jane decided that before going to Vienna, where she was living at the time, she would visit her friends, the Schaeffers in Switzerland.

She said, "The flight across the ocean was dreadful, and the trip from Paris to Geneva, worse. Talk about a tormented person! My mind was at cross purposes. Then as our two-engine plane came in view of the Alps, one of the motors sputtered and coughed, and stopped running, and almost immediately, the steady beat of th the other one was gone too."

"I have never heard a more deathly silence," Jane shuddered at the remembrance. "I had been reading my Bible to try to quiet my mind and had left off on the last few verses in Psalm 119, 'Let my soul live, and it shall praise thee; and let thy judgments help me. I have gone astray like a lost sheep....' In the midst of my thoughts, I heard the click on the inter-com system. As if reading a part in the theater, the stewardess announced: 'Please remain calm. We are having engine trouble.' Seconds later we were told to remove glasses, and the like, and to prepare for a crash landing. It was unreal, like opera, only this time we weren't playing parts.

"Suddenly I realized that shortly I would be standing before my Lord, and I could hear Him asking, 'What have you done for me?' I knew with shame I had little to answer. 'Give me back my life, Lord,' I pleaded, 'and I will really give it to Thee."

An agonizing moment after Jane prayed, one of the motors began to sputter, and not long after, the plane was on the ground, having landed safely with one engine. It took the passengers a few seconds to realize that they were safe, and then a cheer broke out. A few, like Jane, wept silently and thanked God.

Jane's visit to the Schaeffers was timely for them as well as herself. They were going through a crisis and needed help, and so the singer remained with them three weeks. The deep spiritual struggle continued, but now Jane had made a definite promise to God; and though she knew she would be badly misunderstood, she was determined to make the necessary steps to leave opera.

The singer will never forget that day in January, 1960, when she walked slowly along the tree-lined avenue in Vienna on the way to the opera house to tell her manager she was resigning. A sob was locked in her throat. The walk seemed endless. She did, above all, want to put the Lord first, and yet opera was the only life she knew; and she could not imagine what her life would be like without it.

The meeting proved as painful as she had feared. After the usual cordial greeting, she blurted out that she was leaving opera. Her manager thought she was joking or playing a foolish game. Finally, when he realized she was serious, he was horrified. He kept insisting that she take time to think it over, he kept reminding her of all the excellent contracts he had lined up for her; but Jane insisted louder that she was through with opera.

They talked for hours, and Jane had the opportunity to tell this man, whom she respected very much, her entire story — the long search in her life, how she came to believe in the Lord, what she now believed, the reality she found in the Christian faith, and how it was no longer possible to serve two masters. She saw his attitude move from shock to disdain and, at last, to wistfulness. He admitted he had no real purpose in life.

Now the weeks and months of agony were over for Jane. She still had the heartache of being misunderstood by people she loved, and she still had no picture of what her future life would be; but she was again at peace with God.

"As soon as I settled with my manager that I was through with opera," she said, "the Lord gave me quietness — His kind of quietness which is peaceful, hopeful and full of strength."

10. A New Song

In an earlier chapter, you have already been given a glimpse how the Lord is using the opera singer today. Introducing others to good literature is but a small part of the life of Miss Prompt-to-Act. For several years now Jane has been associated with L'Abri Fellowship in Switzerland and works with Dr. and Mrs. Francis A. Schaeffer, whose witness God used to convince her of the reality of the Christian faith. Today the musician is a valued member of the Swiss community — with her love for the Lord and respect for His Word, her many talents, her fluency in four languages, her enthusiasm, her imagination, and her knack for getting things done swiftly and well. "But does she still sing?" is what you want to know. Yes, she does, more than ever today; but she went through a long, hard, dreary time when her only audience was the pots and pans in the kitchen and the heavenly host.

After Jane had the painful interview with her manager in Vienna, she returned to Switzerland. The Schaeffers still desperately needed help with the growing work of L'Abri. She came for a time (so she thought) to do what she could. At this point they did not need a highly trained singer; they needed someone to scrub floors, write letters, carry up supplies from the village, teach Bible classes, wash dishes, shovel snow, make fires, help with the cooking, and one hundred and one other odd jobs. "Odd" jobs indeed for a Southern lady who had been waited upon all her life; but the opera singer plunged into the strange activities with an exuberance, wildness and cheerfulness which helped to make up for her lack of skill in certain areas.

One of the guests at L'Abri, who had recently heard about her conversion, stood watching with fascination as the singer mopped up the steps one morning. As the visitor quickly stepped back in order not to get splashed on, she asked, "What are you going to do now that you've given up your career?"

Without looking up, the singer answered loudly, "I'm doing it!"

Even after Jane moved into Chalet Chesalet, as the hostess there, in the continually expanding work of L'Abri, she still had no place to sing. There were no rooms large enough for a voice trained to sing Wagnerian opera. Around this time, though, Jane did begin the Sunday music hour at Bellevue, the home for children with cerebral palsy, across the road from Chesalet. She brought along her auto-harp, gathered the children around her on the outside terrace, and sang hymns for them in French, German, and English.

She continued to practice as often as she could, gradually acquainting herself with the music of Bach, Handel, Mendelssohn, and other great Christian composers. She still thought her only audience was the Lord and the pots and pans in the kitchen; but when she moved to Chalet Chesalet, she gained another listener, her Swiss neighbor. It was months later that she learned that he often stood with tears in his eyes, in his orchard or with his kitchen windows pushed wide open, listening to the voice coming across the field.

Mr. Lengacher had moved to the tiny village of Huemoz about ten years before the singer arrived in Switzerland. He was by profession a cheese maker, and had had a prosperous business in Geneva. Because of broken health and other sorrows in his life, he had come to the mountains, and there the tall, stooped Swiss-German cut himself off from the French-speaking people of the village. He knew only the companionship of his beloved sheep and bees.

"It was the music," he said, "that changed my life."

The two neighbors became acquainted one day when Jane was working in the garden. From then on they had many good conversations across the fence, and when it drew close to the holidays, she invited him for Christmas dinner along with other guests. Jane wrapped up a German Bible and gave it to her neighbor that Christmas, and the following week he came for a Bible study. And he came again. He had many questions. I believe it was in January that the singer was opening up the book of John for him, and on the same day, he opened his heart to the warmth and love of the Lord Jesus Christ.

Some people grasp the truth more quickly than others, and Mr. Lengacher, like the singer, delights in reading and studying his Bible. Not long after his conversion, he began asking why there was no chapel in connection with L'Abri. Jane explained that they had been praying for one for many years, but they still lacked sufficient money, the land, and, not least of all, the builder.

As time went by and those in the community became better acquainted with Mr. Lengacher (or "the Beeman," as everyone calls him), they learned that he was a man of many talents. One evening when the living room at the Schaeffer's was unusually crowded for the high tea and the Sunday service which followed, the Beeman, stepping among those seated on the floor, measured the width, height, and length of the room. When asked what he was doing, he explained, "I'm going to build a chapel." And he did.

The chapel is the loveliest building on the mountainside. Mr. Lengacher made certain that the ceiling was high enough and the auditorium long enough so that others, besides himself, the pots and pans and the heavenly host, could hear his neighbor sing her praise to the Living Lord. No one who comes to L'Abri these days asks, "Does she still sing?"

Today it would take a book to write about only the musical and artistic side of L'Abri Fellowship. For example: the special concerts given in the chapel with artists from several countries participating; the many tours made by the L'Abri Ensemble; the unusual church services and the part music plays in them; the Music and Art Festivals in England and Switzerland. And then there is the story of how the singer sold her opera costumes to help pay for the chapel. One chapter might tell about Jane's chickens and the thousands of eggs which have been sold to help buy a lovely, little pipe organ for the chapel. There is so much to tell! But what the singer would want you to remember is that she did not know if she would ever sing again after she left the theater. This is all the doing of the Lord. He welcomes praise and song when it is willingly directed to Him.

PART TWO

In Good Company

11. In Good Company

Few in life are spared the agony, at one time or another, of feeling that life is shabby and mean, and that faith in God is dried up. Who hasn't walked heavily through a dark valley, or wept alone because of an inexpressible sorrow? It happens to different people in different ways. To see a loved one suffer innocently can momentarily blot out the reality of one's faith in a God of justice. Being betrayed or hated by someone you love leaves a hollowness which nothing seems to fill.

Simply reading the newspaper and *Time* magazine week after week undermines faith. But nothing — nothing dulls the spirit of a Christian more thoroughly than the unrelenting insistence of TV and the press to keep mankind informed about everything upon, under, and above the earth — *everything* excepting the one thing that could encourage us, the fact that the Lord God is still Lord over all. Rarely are we given this confidence in the news media of today.

A businessman said recently, "It's nonsense the way people think they have to know everything today. They end up knowing nothing. If most of us were as faithful about studying our Bibles as we are listening to the news, we'd be experiencing revival right now."

Not obeying God, we turn ourselves from Him; and how dim the Creator becomes when we long for something or someone over the years and our prayers do not seem to be answered. There are many ways to break the communication between man and God, and as John Newton told a friend who thought that God had deserted him, "You are in good company."

Books have been written about Job, but all I wish to recall

right now is his despairing cry, "O that I knew where I might find Him." It also helps to remember that both Isaiah and Jeremiah thought they had lost touch with God at critical moments in their lives. Life is not as comprehensive and expressible as some would have us believe, and the most mysterious and memorable lament of all are the words of the Lord Jesus Christ from the cross, "My God, my God, why hast thou forsaken me?"

We are indeed in good company, those of us who waver once in a while. Strong faith does not run in a straight line. It is more apt to jog up and down. Robert Browning in a moment of ecstasy wrote, "Oh, the wild joys of living! the leaping from rock to rock!" Then undoubtedly he had a few mornings when he felt more inclined to throw rocks. It is part of the total experience. We are up, we're down; and as it is expressed in the spiritual, "Nobody knows the trouble I've seen," sometimes we're nearly to the ground. What is amazing though — I might feel out of God's presence, but God has not left me if I am His child through faith in Christ.

An older friend told me how he battled with his bouts of depression. "I've learned to ride them out," he said. "It's like being in a fog. You can't see the bow of the ship, but everything is there, nevertheless — the sea, the sky, the sun, other ships. You learn to creep along. The worst thing is to sit still. And it doesn't hurt to make noise. The other fellow can't see you, but he can hear you."

It is gain to learn to ride out our troubles. So we have a few hard days; that does not change the promises of God. He is for us whether we are up or down, and when we are ready to receive help, He will heal our broken hearts and bind up our wounds. While waiting for comfort, it never hurts to recall the words of Paul, another in the good company acquainted with despair, "I reckon that the sufferings of this present time are not worthy to be compared with the glory which shall be revealed in us" (Rom. 8:18).

A few years ago, someone close to me, a grandmother, lost

her husband. Her sorrow was deep and it seemed impossible for her to go on; but one of her grandchildren helped her to see that we owe it to others to go on bravely, yea, eventually even cheerfully, in spite of crushed hopes and dreams.

"Grandma," the child suddenly said one day as we were riding in the country, "you're going to be in a wheelchair soon, you're so old and sad looking."

Today this grandmother is a true comfort and joy to her grandchildren and many others in her town, because she has learned one of the deepest lessons Christ taught us: that we are in the world to love and serve God and others. We cannot do it when we are turned inward viewing our sorrow. I know this widow had to force a smile in those first long months she was learning to walk alone with God, but the Lord rewarded her effort. As she brings happiness to others, He reveals more of Himself.

12. Need All Three

The youngest son in a family was asked to say the blessing at breakfast one morning. With his head bowed low, he prayed in a clear, loud voice,

"We thank Thee, God, for this beautiful day and for our food. Amen."

Everyone at the table glared at him. It was a miserable day, cold, damp, and dark. His father said sternly that he must never pray insincerely. An older brother muttered, "What a jerk!" And his mother asked, "What do you mean, dear, a beautiful day?"

As the youngster reached in front of his brother for the strawberry jam, he said simply, "You can never judge a day by its weather."

A friend was telling me that he has an aunt who never permits anyone to speak unfavorably in her home about the weather. She begins her days (and the days start early on a Kansas farm) recalling that this is the day the Lord has made, let us rejoice and be glad in it, and with the stubbornness of a lady born in Germany who has lived close to God for at least seventy years, she learned long ago that it is indeed foolish to judge a day by its weather.

Nor should we judge people simply by what we see. A few years ago I lived in a wooded area in the country, a startling contrast from Chicago where I had spent one year. It was so quiet at night you could hear an ant walk across the floor; but you usually didn't, because the ants, like the country folk, go to bed early. The small, white frame house was surrounded by trees, grass, squirrels, daisies, chipmunks, birds, clover, rabbits, and very determined weeds. I enjoyed being there.

After a while I noticed that my visitors responded to the setting in one of three ways. There were those who smiled when they saw the friendly house hiding in the woods and weeds at the end of the lane. "Aren't the trees beautiful," they'd say. "And the daisies, I love them. I don't know if I've ever seen them growing all over a yard before." Then they'd usually sigh and say something like, "Must be grand to live here."

Then quite a few of my friends could be grouped in category two. "Good grief, can't you afford a lawn mower?" they'd say. "It must be damp and dreary living in the woods. Eek! — there's another big, black ant! How can you stand it, it's so quiet here! Wouldn't surprise me if you get snowed in next winter. The plows never come down these little lanes."

And, of course, like you, I have one or two friends who do not register one way or the other. You never do know what they are thinking. This is group three, those so absorbed in their own problems (or success) that they are incapable of responding to another person's life or of reacting to different surroundings.

What's so nice in life is that we need all three types. There's room for everybody; and would that we'd remember it and stop trying to crowd "the different ones" off the edge of the earth. I have observed that most of us like the bright and hopeful people the best. They are easier to have around; but that does not mean we do not need the suggesters and fault-finders. There would be no progress in the world apart from them. So let's give thanks to all those in category two. Think how unruly it would get if everyone liked daisies and clover in their yards.

And what about group three? Those who are absorbed in themselves. Well, while we are praying for them, we can also be reminded that but for the grace of God, there go I. No one gets out of himself until he sees beyond himself, and that requires help from above.

How nicely it would all work out if we'd only remember more often to let the weather and people be themselves. Each day is different, and each one of us has our role to play in time which we alone can accomplish; and *if nothing else,* some of us less conventional folk can always serve as poor examples to the rest of mankind. The wonder is that God cares for any of us. As the German lady who lives on the Kansas farm once said to her nephew, "I have never ceased to marvel at John 3:16, 'For God so loved the world, that he gave his only begotten Son, that whosoever believeth in him should not perish, but have everlasting life.'"

And the following verse should also be held in front of our eyes as we critically peer at one another while walking through life: "For God sent not his Son into the world to condemn the world; but that the world through him might be saved." How can we not love and give thanks for such a Saviour?

13. See for Yourself

She is in a nursing home, a charming, delicate, unhappy lady with a record of careless living in the past. When a young minister called the other day, he began the conversation, "And what is your trouble?"

"I have so many, young man," she snapped, "I don't think it's worth beginning the story."

And that was the end of conversation, or that is what she said. I suspect she got in a few more comments. Later in the evening, when she was telling about her visitor and his question, she laughed. It wasn't a mean laugh, though somewhat brittle. We talked about many things, and when it was nearly time to leave, my friend surprisingly asked me to read a Psalm. Generally she waved away the Bible. But before I could find the place, she had a few more things to say about the young minister — "Imagine, asking what is my trouble! You'd think the clergy would know that the one thing we want in a place like this is to forget our troubles! That's why I want you to read from the Bible. Go ahead, go ahead," she said irritably. "It used to help me."

I began reading Psalm 107. "Oh, that men would praise the Lord for his goodness, and for his wonderful works to the children of men! For he satisfieth the longing soul, and filleth the hungry with goodness...."

We sat quietly for a moment after the reading. My sick friend in her dainty, pink bed jacket and carefully arranged silver-gray hair was looking out of the window. When she finally spoke, her voice came from far away,

"You seem to enjoy your faith. I wish I did. I never have,

really. Oh, I went to church and all that, but since I've been here, it's almost as if I had no faith."

The room was hot, with a slight odor of disinfectant and boiled cabbage; a fan was blowing noisily, and mixed with that was an ugly blur from the confusion of several TV sets turned on in nearby rooms. She added huskily, "Peace. That's something else I surely don't have."

The closing bell rang, and we did not get to continue the conversation; but my thoughts dwelled on it and on her as I drove home. She asked a real question, a disturbing one, a question that cannot be answered lightly or carelessly. Can an older person in a crowded nursing home, who has lived most of her life selfishly, can such a person know the peace of God? Is it too late?

A person with my limitations has no adequate response, but the answer in Scripture, the true Word of God, is ringing with hope, "Saith the Lord, Turn ye even to me with all your heart ... and I will restore to you the years that the locust hath eaten" (Joel 2:12, 25).

Those are great words of encouragement and comfort, never to be treated lightly. They are not spoken by a mere man, but by the Creator-Redeemer God of the whole universe who is able to satisfy every longing, lonely soul.

The peace which God gives is His. It has nothing to do with who we are, where we are, how old we are. We don't make peace with God. It has already been made. Paul expressed it plainly in Colossians 1:20, "And, having made peace through the blood of his cross...." It is only the Lord who can say to us, "My peace I give unto you," and the way to make it yours, even in a crowded, noisy nursing home, is to accept the gift.

As one of my friends in another nursing home frequently says about the gifts God pours down upon His children, "It never hurts to add, thank You, Lord, thank You."

There is, of course, a condition to be fulfilled before we can receive God's gift of peace. All God's promises to the children of men are conditional; and may I add, they are all reasonable and fair. In this case, all the Lord asks is, "Turn to Me. Turn to Me and I will give My peace." It is perfectly reasonable, perfectly fair. Why should God give peace to someone more interested in following the ways of the world, or to someone who doesn't believe He is there?

As long as my friend, the fragile, but wayward lady in the nursing home tries to excuse away her behavior in the years gone by, and her present state of being out of fellowship with the Living Lord, and does not humbly ask for the cleansing power of the Saviour, she cannot hope to be peaceful. His peace is real, but it can never be experienced until we fulfill God's condition: "Turn to Me."

Those who know the peace of God are the ones who have turned to Him. And what deep peace have they who go farther and turn to God with all their heart. In this setting the Christian faith can be enjoyed in a nursing home, a hospital, a prison, a room in the slums, a palace, at home, and abroad.

It is only after we have turned to the Lord that we learn He is all for us and will do exactly what He has promised, "I will restore to you the years that the locust hath eaten."

Some of the most joyful Christians I know and have read about are those who have taken Christ into their lives after years of living apart from Him. They know, they really know what a marvelous thing it is to be peaceful. It is never too late to turn to God, and know the beauty of redemption.

"Oh, give thanks unto the Lord, for he is good: for his mercy endureth for ever! Let the redeemed of the Lord say so, whom he hath redeemed from the hand of the enemy. . . ."

Yesterday I stopped again to see my friend in the nursing home. She was reading her Bible. She had just finished all of Psalm 107, and was trying to find the part about the locust. "Not that I don't believe you," she winked, "but I want to **find** out these things for myself."

14. SMASHCRASH!!

There is something in the human heart that likes violence, chaos, and something to be against. Dylan Thomas expressed the paradox in the simple words of a mother talking to her child, "Oh, isn't life a terrible thing, thank God?"

The themes children write in school illustrate the point. I borrowed the following from the notebook of one of my nephews. It is entitled, "BANG!"

"Someday I would like to see a car carrier driving down the street have one of its chains bust and SMASHCRASH!! A brand new eight-million-dollar Lincoln Continental fall off. And better yet, have it fall on another Lincoln Continental. That would really be a mess."

The other day I was reading about a strange situation. Two meetings were held two weeks apart in a certain church. The first was a farewell party for a missionary and his wife going to Africa. Two weeks later, the neighbors in the community were called to the same church building to protest the moving into their neighborhood of a Negro family. This is a strange situation, I thought. Two white people are expected by the power and spirit of the Lord Jesus Christ to walk among millions of black people and extend his love, whereas the six hundred members of the home church cannot gather enough love among themselves to include one Negro family.

A part of wisdom is in knowing what to be against, and it impresses me that not all persons make the right choice. It takes relatively the same amount of energy for Mike Leary to argue with his wife every night as it did for Martin Luther to contend for truth.

By nature Luther was not too different from ourselves, a man of deep passion; but with Christ in his life, it was turned to good. God used Martin Luther in the battle all Christians should be fighting — the war against evil, ignorance, superstition. As Paul wrote, "We wrestle not against flesh and blood, but against principalities, against powers, against the rulers of the darkness of this world, against spiritual wickedness in high places" (Eph. 6:12).

The petty fights, sometimes terrible battles, which rage day in and day out between employers and employees, politicians, nations, individuals, and between the members of a church, are shocking evidence that many persons have not learned what to be against. Riots in the streets, violence in big cities, rebellion in universities and colleges, all testify to the waywardness of the natural heart unbridled by the Holy Spirit. The only hope is to take on the whole armor of God, that we may be able to withstand in the evil day, and, as Paul says, "having done all, to stand" (Eph. 6:13).

The real heroes in history are not those who fought against their fellow man, but those who drew their swords against oppression, hate, and blasphemy. We're always going to be against something in life, some more than others; but let us make certain that what we are *against* is *for* a worthy cause.

15. Look Beyond

I like the way children write. Here is an essay by an eight-year-old child.

"A grandmother is a lady who has no children of her own, so she likes other people's boys and girls. Grandmas don't have anything to do except be there. If they take us for walks they slow down past pretty leaves and caterpillars. They never say, 'Hurry up.' Usually they are fat but not too fat to tie shoes. They wear glasses, and sometimes they can take their teeth out.

"They can answer questions like why dogs hate cats and why God isn't married. They don't talk visitors' talk like visitors do which is hard to understand. When they read to us they don't skip words or mind if it is the same story again.

"Everybody should try to have a grandma, especially if you don't have television, because grandmas are the only grown-ups who always have time."

Happily, there are many grandmothers in the world as wonderful as this child's grandmother — who take time with their children's children, who are looking beyond and giving these little ones real food for their souls. I know one grandmother who has taken a course in story telling "so I can make the Bible more exciting for my grandchildren," she explained. "I used to play games with the youngsters when they'd come and spend a night, but since I've improved my story telling technique, they want stories instead of games." She smiled, "I've never pored over the Bible in my whole life as I have in the past year, and it gets more interesting to me every time I pick it up."

I asked her how she studied the Bible.

"I use all the help I can get," she said. "I'm no scholar. I'm thankful for every word Matthew Henry wrote, as well as Spurgeon, F. B. Meyer, G. Campbell Morgan and Martin Luther. Then I use modern translations and paraphrases. They are such a help."

We didn't get much farther with our talk, because the house began to fill up with children.

"All these are your grandchildren?" I asked.

"Oh, no," she laughed. "They asked last week if they could invite a few friends, and I see they have!"

As it said in the essay, "Everybody should try to have a grandma"; a grandmother like my friend who is sharing the best she knows with her grandchildren and their friends. It was Phillip Brooks who wrote,

"Certainly, in our own little sphere it is not the most active people to whom we owe the most. It is the lives, like the stars, which simply pour down on us the calm light of their bright and faithful being, up to which we look and out of which we gather the deepest calm and courage.... No man or woman of the humblest sort can really be strong, gentle, pure, and good, without the world being better for it, without somebody being helped and comforted by the very existence of that goodness." I am thankful I had grandmothers like that who always had time for the little ones.

16. Please Forgive My Swedish

At the turn of the century, about the time of that new-fangled contraption, the telephone, Grandpa would holler, "Tyst barn, Chicago kalla!" (That's Swedish for "Quiet, children, Chicago is calling!") My mother was living on a farm in northern Illinois with her mother and father and eight brothers and sisters. It was back in the days when one "tyst" could quiet all the children around the table.

One summer the family had an exciting visit from a relative who lived in California. Everyone enjoyed the visit of Cousin Claus; and he promised the children he would send them something special when he returned to the fabulous land of lemons and oranges.

Several months passed after Cousin Claus left the Illinois farm. Then one day Grandma received a postcard from the Cherry Valley train depot: "This is to notify you that a package has arrived from California."

After the card had been passed around the table, Grandpa put on his store-bought glasses and studied it.

"Ja," he said (and please forgive my Swedish), "det är bäst vi tar lumbar vagn." (That's supposed to mean, "Yes, it's best we take the lumber wagon.")

One of the boys rushed out to the barn to hitch up the plump horses, and Grandpa and his sons went off to Cherry Valley to fetch the package or packages. When they returned in a short while and the boys were red in the face from laughing. Grandpa, with a solemn face and wide gesture of his hand, presented Grandma with a box about the width and length of a credit card. In it were two miniature spoons.

Yesterday when I was told that I had a parcel at the village post office, not owning a "lumbar vagn," I persuaded the friend who lives with me to take a walk down the hill. Later as we pushed, pulled and dragged a huge carton of dishes up the mountainside, we wished the package contained only a couple of spoons.

That same evening, however, when we set the table for the Sunday morning breakfast guests we were glad not to have to use a chipped blue-striped saucer with a cracked cup decorated in red roses. Quite a few dishes get broken in our chalet in the course of a year, but dishes can always be replaced. If one person in every hundred who visits this community finds hope and meaning for his or her life, it is worth an entire "lumbar vagn" of chipped cups, cracked saucers and broken plates. It was the Lord Himself who said, "I say unto you, there is joy in the presence of the angels of God over one sinner that repenteth" (Luke 15:10).

17. An Expensive Tree

"That tree has to go," she said. The singer and I were standing in the garden, picking the last of the spinach before winter and looking up at the large, dead nut tree which was leaning toward the chalet. We had put off calling the nursery, because it is expensive to have a tree cut down, and with Christmas not far off, well....

We thought of asking one of the young men studying in Farel House to chop it down. They can do most anything. We considered some of the other people living in this Swiss community known as L'Abri Fellowship, and as amazing and varied as their talents are, we decided it might not include chopping down trees. The only alternative was to hire a professional woodsman. Even though the chalet has weathered wind, sleet, and heavy snow in its 250-year history, it might do it no good to have a tree fall on it now.

It took several phone calls, but finally one day the woodcutter appeared at our door. Only recently I had been in Illinois where thousands of elm trees have died and was painfully aware how expensive it is to remove a tree. So the first thing we wished to know was how much it was going to cost; and if too much, we would wait until after Christmas. We were taking the chance, of course, that in the meantime the tree might fall on the tile roof and give us even more to think about.

We had called in our neighbor to translate. We both knew some French, but in a business transaction, it's best to know for sure what is going on. The round, jovial woodcutter walked around the tree, measured it, gave it a few pats, all the time talking to our Swiss neighbor. I followed very little of what they were saying, but suddenly my ears picked up "600 francs." In the meantime, my American friend, who shares the chalet *and* expenses with me, also understood, "600 francs."

Frantically we calculated how much that was in dollars. She whispered, "That's about 150 dollars."

It seemed like an enormous amount of money to have to spend just before Christmas. Then when I thought I understood the woodcutter to say he was taking the trunk and leaving us the branches, I shook my head. Jane looked as unhappy as I felt.

Our Swiss neighbor looked puzzled. She took us aside and said in French, "It is really a very good price, at least 200 francs more than I thought he would offer."

Jane caught it quicker than I. She asked guardedly, "What do you mean, *he* is offering *us?*"

Then, as if the dead tree had fallen on both of us, we got it. The nursery man was *buying* our tree!!! He was giving *us* 600 francs, and part of the bargain was to chop up the branches for us to burn in the fireplace.

It occurred to me afterwards that this was similar to my attitude before I received Christ as my Saviour. I was convinced I couldn't afford it. It involved giving up too much. It was only after I entered into the transaction that I discovered what a gift I had received.

Today we planted a new tree in the place of the dead one, a weeping willow. As I frequently look down from the balcony upon that fragile touch of gold on the green mountainside, I hope it will always remind me to be thankful for the new life which God has given me in Christ Jesus.

If for any reason you are uncertain whether or not you have received the precious gift of salvation, you can be sure today. Your part is to come, to receive, and to be thankful. Come just as you are. Many people think they have to wait until they are ready. "I'm not good enough to be a Christian." You hear it all the time, but those saying it have missed the point. No one is good enough. God invites us as we are. He will change us, if we need changing. The words of Charlotte Elliott's poem are for all of us who long for peace with God and a quiet mind:

> Just as I am, without one plea,
> But that Thy blood was shed for me,
> And that Thou bidd'st me come to Thee,
>   O Lamb of God, I come, I come!
>
> Just as I am, though tossed about
> With many a conflict, many a doubt,
> Fightings and fears within. without,
>   O Lamb of God, I come, I come!
>
> Just as I am, Thou wilt receive,
> Wilt welcome, pardon, cleanse, relieve;
> Because Thy promise I believe,
>   O Lamb of God, I come, I come!

18. Five or Four Miles Away

I have a letter which I treasure. It was not written to me. It was sent to a close friend of mine, and I asked if I could copy it. My friend, who is blessed with energy and a cheerful disposition, has been going about doing good for years. At one time she was teaching swimming in a Y.M.C.A. in Michigan. Besides the regular classes, Dorothy Ann had two special groups. One was for blind children, and the other for a group of youngsters who were mentally retarded.

Teaching the children without sight to swim was exhilarating. One of the tragedies in being blind is that you always have to move cautiously, but in the water the blind children thrashed their legs and splashed their arms with the same abandon as those with sight. And there was always their teacher's reassuring voice and arms which dared them to try things they never dreamed possible.

But I think Dorothy Ann enjoyed the mentally retarded class even more than did the youngsters. They were the most good-natured, rollicking children with whom she had ever worked. She told me, "These children were so uncomplicated and happy. It taught me one thing — no, two. God makes up for every loss; and never pity another person and his problems. He may be better off than you realize."

In response to the least thing she did for the children, they would hug her, splash on her, or telephone her any hour of the day or night to tell her they loved her. Then there was Kitty, whose smiling little face and neat appearance scarcely betrayed the damage done to her brain at birth. She was a favorite. And Kitty had never met *anyone* like teacher.

Almost the same time that Dorothy Ann and her family moved away from Michigan, the welfare board felt it was best for Kitty to be put in the state hospital. Her home situation was poor, and as she was growing older, her problems were increasing. It was the only answer to a hard question. Shortly after she was taken to the institution, she wrote the following letter to my friend, now living hundreds of miles from Michigan:
"Dear Teacher,

Guess what I am at Coldwater Hospital, but there isant nothing rong with me. They said to come down here, I don't know why they wanted me to, but they did. I dident want to come. Would you, by the way, have you ever been here. I dont care much about it. Only thing I like about it is that it's right near you. You know, you can probably come and see me. It's not far, I imagine, O, about five or four miles away from your house.

T H A N K   Y O U

Love,
Kitty"

It is true and we all know it. There are some days when we seem unable to find happiness. But

O God, remind us that there is rarely a time when we cannot give a little happiness to someone near or far. Cause even people like us, often full of sound and fury, self-pity and lust, to increase and abound in love one to another, and toward all men, particularly those less fortunate than ourselves, those who live five or four miles away. May we learn and live-out the reality of these words:

"Pure religion and undefiled before God and the Father is this, To visit the fatherless and widows in their affliction, and To keep unspotted from the world.... Whosoever will be chief among you, let him be your servant; Even as the Son of man came not to be ministered unto, but to minister, and to give his life a ransom for many.... I have given you an example

....The servant is not greater than his Lord....If ye know these things, happy are ye if ye do them."
(James 1:7; Matthew 20:28; John 13:16, 17)

19. Back to Adam and Eve

The nights in the Swiss Alps never seem as dark as in a large city. Even when there is only a sliver of the moon, it is possible to walk along a path without a flashlight. Last night I stopped to look at one of the lower, gentle slopes in front of our mountain range. It recalled to my mind a prayer meeting I had read about which took place in Wales.

One evening, early in the Spring of 1903, four young men were discovered on a mountain near the place called Cefnhirgoed, holding a prayer meeting. They had been there every night for a month. And their object? To plead with God to revive His work.

A friend who discovered them joined in. The informal meetings continued until the members of the church were stirred by the fact that their case was being pleaded before God by a group of teen-agers. There were others who looked on the spectacle with suspicion (These are the adults who can never believe youth is up to any good!), and there were many who were sure it was only a passing thing. But the young men prayed on.

In the second month, more people came out to the mountainside to see what was going on. To the amazement of the minister, many of the curious remained to pray also. The number increased every night, and as the group grew larger, so did the fervor. At last the spark ignited the entire church, and as their pastor described it,

"We were moved with the spirit of prayer and with a passion for souls. The neighborhood was soon ablaze with the divine fire; and the meetings which at first were attended by only four were now frequented by scores. All testified to the power of God in a special manner."

Something like this is stirring in the west-end of my hometown. Recently a church burned down, I mean, burned down to the ground. A friend wrote,

"We had been trying to have one hundred in our prayer meetings for months, but the best we could get were fifty to about seventy. Well, last night, packed into the little youth building, the only part of the church which still stands, we had over one hundred!"

Yes, indeed, this is when religion gets exciting — out in the fresh air or when the church burns down! If this seems too strenuous, though, it is well to remember that God will hear us *even from within* our comfortable churches, if we pray aright. We have been taught what to pray; we simply need to remember to believe it and do it.

"If my people, which are called by my name, shall humble themselves, and pray, and seek my face, and turn from their wicked ways; then will I hear from heaven, and will forgive their sin, and will heal their land" (II Chron. 7:14).

The friend, who wrote about her church burning down, has spent the greater part of her time the last few years in bed. From this unique pulpit she carries on a more spirited mission program than many entire churches. At the present moment she is corresponding with missionaries in Hong Kong, South America, Africa, Taiwan, Alaska, Morocco, the Philippines, Switzerland, and Florida, Iowa, and Chicago. In several of the places mentioned, she writes to more than one person, and without meaning to, I've probably left out a few countries. Often her letters are written at 5:30 A.M. or 3:30. When their neighbor goes out at dawn to milk the cows, he often meets Gladys' husband going to work. "Well, I see Gladys is writing letters again," the farmer smiles as he sees the light streaming from the bedroom of their small house. "Doesn't she ever get tired of writing?"

I am sure she gets tired, but Gladys has accepted this as a gift of God to be able to encourage others. Rather than lie sleepless and concentrate on her pain and other problems, she has learned that the hours pass quickly when thinking of others. Rarely do her letters mention her illness. Actually they are hymns of praise to God, her Lord and Saviour, who has reached down and given her happiness and an overflowing heart in the midst of her personal difficulties. He has taught her the simple lesson that it is impossible to write cheerfully and hopefully to others without being encouraged yourself.

This is only part of the missionary program of Gladys Shipley. Every morning before her grandchildren (who live in the same neighborhood) go to school, they stop by at Grandma's house for a prayer meeting. I am honored to say that two of these children are my personal "prayer warriors," and, believe me, I have many days when I'm thankful the warriors are praying.

The faith of Gladys reminds me of Dwight L. Moody. It is as simple and direct. He too never let a small thing like a lack of a formal education stand in his way. Moody shared with the entire world what God had taught him through his diligent and enthusiastic study of the Bible. And this is the way it is with my friend. I would far rather have her Godly wisdom than all the learning in the world which discounts the true and living God.

Gladys is like Moody in another way. She never wastes time. Each person is a new challenge, and it might be her only opportunity to tell of her Lord. Last week while her husband was talking on the phone, the paper boy came to the front door. Gladys called from the bedroom and asked the youngster to come in. She told him that her husband would pay him as soon as he finished his call. She started to tell the boy about her church burning down — "But that doesn't change Jesus Christ," she said. "He is the same today, yesterday, and forever."

In conversing with him she learned many things about him, and at the right moment, Gladys asked, with gentleness, "Sonny, do you know Jesus as your Saviour and Lord?"

He replied earnestly,

"I don't rightly know, Ma'am, if I do or not."

"Well," Gladys wrote, "I took him clear back to Adam and Eve...." And knowing her thoroughness, I am sure that young newsboy will never be able to say on the day of Judgment, "I never heard that the Bible was written for me. No one ever told me that I, too, may walk with God here on earth."

When the boy left the house, Gladys made sure that he had a Bible; and she marked several important parts he should read first. And, of course, she also told him that we would ALL be praying for him — the prayer warriors and the rest of us in Hong Kong, South America, Africa, Taiwan, Alaska, Morocco, the Philippines, Switzerland, and Florida, Iowa, and Chicago.

"I believe in a faith that you can see," said Moody, "a living, working faith that prompts to action." I do too, and it gives me pleasure to tell you about my adventure-loving friend in Winnebago who is in loving touch with the whole world from her small bedroom. It is as the Lord Jesus Christ told us: "Give, and it shall be given unto you; good measure, pressed down, and shaken together, and running over, shall men give into your bosom. For with the same measure that ye mete withal it shall be measured to you again" (Luke 6:38).

20. Live Today

A young man was hiking in a wild, wooded area in Canada. It was Spring and he had that careless, exceedingly alive feeling which seems to go with the season. He was carrying no weapons. All he had was a camera. He walked past the entrance to a cave. Then he backed up. He couldn't see anything in the cave, but thought it might make an interesting picture. He stood very still as he steadied the camera and pointed it into the black, yawning cavern.

He didn't get around to developing his film for several weeks, and he had almost forgotten that singular day in May when he walked in the woods as one who had not a care in the world. When he picked up the cave picture, he gulped. All he had seen was blackness when he peered into the cave; but the sensitive lens of his camera had recorded a good-sized lynx crouching in the shadow, ready to spring upon him had he taken even one step closer.

Is this not an accurate picture of life? Its uncertainties, mysteries, surprises, both good and bad. Every human being lives within the framework of not knowing what is going to happen tomorrow. For me, the remembrance of this makes me want to do the best I can, by the grace of God, right this day. Some people might think it morbid to dwell on the brevity of life. But I don't mean it in that spirit. I'm thinking of it in just the opposite way: Isn't it wonderful to be alive today? Give me a song in my heart, O Lord, for this day.

God often gives us the best songs when the going is rough on all sides. A young friend of mine had a terrible struggle coming to believe in Christ. The battle for her soul went on for years, and the day she became a Christian was a day of rejoicing for many of us. And now, only a few months after her conversion, she is seriously ill. Our first thoughts when we heard she was in the hospital, "Will her faith stand the test?"

As the reports have come to us, it has been a time of rejoicing again. The Lord has truly given her a song in the night. As one of her friends told us, "The whole hospital is talking about the courage and faith of Angela! I'm more convinced than ever, myself, that trusting Christ is the only way to live."

No one knows what a day will bring forth, but if the Lord is in the day and acknowledged as your Lord and my Lord, we'll be able to stand. It reminds me of a story some one told me last week. After a wild storm, a man was walking in his garden to observe the damage done to his property. On the path he found a torn nest. He looked down at the wreckage and pitied the poor birds. As he stood there thinking of the unfortunate creatures, he heard some activity and twittering over his head. The birds were building another nest.

In Chapter 6 of Matthew, beginning with verse 25 to the end, my Bible has this heading: "The cure of anxiety: trust in the Father's care." Here is the Christian prescription for living a life of song even today, no matter what the circumstances are:

(It is the Good Shepherd speaking to all those who will listen) —

> "Therefore I say unto you,
> Take no thought for your life,
> what ye shall eat, or what ye shall
> drink; nor yet for your body, what
> ye shall put on. Is not the life more
> than meat, and the body than
> raiment?
> Behold the fowls of the air:
> for they sow not, neither do they
> reap, nor gather into barns; yet

your heavenly Father feedeth them.
Are ye not much better than they? . . .
Take therefore no thought for
the morrow: for the morrow shall
take thought for the things of itself.
Sufficient unto the day is the evil
thereof." — Matthew 6:25, 26, 34

PART THREE

"Joy Is Wisdom"

21. "Joy Is Wisdom"

A few of us were talking together one afternoon about this and that, when a mother, who is interested in better understanding the times in which we live, suddenly asked, "Do you think wisdom can be learned, I mean, the way you learn to drive a car or a new language or how to fill out your income tax forms?"

It is not an unimportant question. Nearly every day of our lives we run into situations where, if only we had used greater wisdom (or even a little) we wouldn't be in the predicament we find ourselves at the moment. It takes wisdom to hold down a job, to be a good parent, to teach as well as learn from others, to live happily though rich, to live richly though poor; and it requires extra wisdom to live peacefully with one's relatives, friends, and neighbors — not even to mention the reservoir of wisdom it takes to go on cheerfully when the plumbing clogs up or the car won't start when you're on the way to an important engagement.

Before we can decide whether or not wisdom can be learned, it must be defined. An older Swiss friend, who is a very wise man, is convinced that patience is wisdom. Who can deny that it surely is a big part of it? Alexandre Dumas had somewhat the same idea. He said that all human wisdom can be summed up in two words — wait and hope. The poet, William Butler Yeats, had a lovely idea about wisdom. He spoke of "joy as wisdom," or it could be said the other way, "wisdom is joy." It's something to think about.

People today think they "know" so much because of the advances in such areas as science, medicine, and technology;

but simply *to know,* is that wisdom? An author and scientist, who has little use for Christianity, said recently, "No one knows more about our world today than our young people." (A grandmother commenting on this statement said, "You surely don't know much if you don't know who made the world!") Those who look around at the world and make their pompous statements as if there is no God, no Bible, no absolutes, no sin, no sinners, and no cross, display the sort of foolishness Paul speaks about in Romans 1:22: "... claiming themselves to be wise about God, they became utter fools instead."

Anyone can line up a bunch of facts in their heads about the world in which we live, but until those proud, full heads bow before the Creator who made the world and themselves, they are not wise. Webster's dictionary says that wisdom is the power of judging rightly and following the soundest course of action, based on knowledge, experience, understanding....

Job tops all the definitions of wisdom in these few words: "Behold, the fear [or reverence] of the Lord, that is wisdom; and to depart from evil is understanding" (Job 28:28)

Even though millions upon millions of Bibles have been printed since the Reformation, we stand in the same position as Martin Luther in his day. He re-discovered the Bible, and it transformed his life and the world which followed. When I think of what Luther knew and had done with his life by the time he was twenty-four, it puts all of us to shame; and yet this man of genius, amazing energy, talent and character, when he learned about Christ, said, "The desire of self-justification is the cause of all the distresses of the heart.... Faith in Christ takes away from you all trust in your own wisdom, righteousness, and strength; it teaches you that if Christ had not died for you, and had not thus saved you, neither you nor any other creature would have been able to do it.... Now Christ is the one, sole, and true God. When you have Him for your God, you have not other gods."

We in the twentieth century need to re-discover the Bible, too. Like Luther, our hearts need to be led back to the Lamb of God who takes away the sin of the world. There was no generation gap between Luther and the youth of his day because of the firmness with which he relied upon the Holy Scriptures and which gave to his teaching great authority. People not only heard his clear, sound words, but saw them in action too. Melanchthon said that Luther drew sinners to Christ by the holiness of his life. Of course, a young person learns to hate religion when his father, an elder in the church, is a mean, hard drinking, selfish man. Young people have the right to say, "Show me the way, and I'll follow."

The mother who asked if wisdom can be learned has already opened the door. James said that it is a question of asking: "If any of you lack wisdom, let him ask of God, that giveth to all men liberally.... But ask in faith, nothing wavering" (James 1:5, 6).

22. *A Wise, Old Man*

Do you have trouble getting along with people? Perhaps this story can help you:

A certain man arrived at the gates of an ancient town. He saw an old man drowsing on a bench with his head pillowed against the sun-baked wall.

"Old man," he shouted, "what are the people like in this town? I'm planning to move here, and it is of interest to me to know what sort of people shall be my new neighbors."

The old man slowly shifted his feet and with his eyes closed asked quietly, "What were the people like in the city from which you came?"

The younger man impatiently jerked the basket from his back and dropped down on the bench beside the old man.

"Whew, I'm done in. That's a tiresome walk from Termoli." He reached in his basket and drew out a bottle from which he drank noisily. Finally he said, "So you want to know what the people are like in Termoli?"

He laughed bitterly, "Thank God I'm getting out of that hole. They're a pack of cheats and no-goods. Wasn't a decent man where I worked, and my wife will tell you the same thing. She was always having a run-in with one of our neighbors!"

He grinned sourly, "She's mighty good at telling them off. She even had a fight with the head soldier on our wall one night when he informed her that she was violating some stupid, local law. I tell you, old man, I wouldn't go back to Termoli for all the marble in Rome. It's a stinking place."

The old man opened his eyes and looked directly at the younger man, "It's the same here, my son; awful people. You will find only cheats and no-goods; and I am certain that your wife will find her neighbors difficult, and the local laws, stupid."

A few weeks later, another man came from Termoli and stopped by the old man nodding in the sun near the gate of the town.

"Pardon me, sir," he said as he bowed to the old man. "I am soon moving to your community, and I should appreciate hearing your opinion about the people in your town."

The old man opened his eyes, "Sit down, my boy. You must be weary after the hot, dusty walk from Termoli."

"Thank you, sir, that is kind of you. It is a warm hike, but the time passed pleasantly as I recited favorite chapters from the Scripture. As a boy, my grandfather urged me to memorize the things that are true and the things that are beautiful."

"Were there others in Termoli like your grandfather?" the old man asked.

"Yes, that was a wonderful place to live, sir," the younger man said with enthusiasm. "We lived in a very humble neighborhood, but we were rich with friends. I left my dear wife in tears, because she is so unhappy about leaving our town."

The wise old man looked into the eyes of the younger man and said, "You tell your wife to dry her tears. She will soon have many precious friends in Angoli, because the people in this place are very much like the people you have described in Termoli."

If you want to get along with people, invite the Lord Jesus into your life. He is the only one who can equip us to live with others, by changing us so we can live with ourselves. As Peter said,

"And now this word to each of you: be as one big family, full of sympathy towards each other; full of love for one another with tender hearts and humble minds. Don't repay evil for evil. Don't snap back at those who say unkind things about you. Instead, pray for God's help for them, for we are to be kind to others, and God will bless us for it. If you want a happy, good life, keep control of your tongue, and guard your lips from telling lies. Turn away from evil and do good; try to live in peace even if you must run after it to catch and hold it! For the Lord is watching His children, listening to their prayers; but the Lord's face is hard against those who do evil." (I Peter 3:8-12 *Living Letters*)

23. Pinched Faith

According to surveys, doctors' charts, and what you hear at coffee parties, tens of thousands of persons go through life feeling tired and run-down. Physicians say that most people feel tired and run-down because they *are* tired and run-down.

Modern man gets old before he ought to, because he goes to bed after midnight and disrupts his sleep with a shrill alarm clock, rushes to work to punch the time clock, runs across the street to the drugstore at the coffee break, and so forth. It makes me tired to talk about it.

It is possible that some of the tiredness of our age is related to the pinched quality of our faith. "With God, the most of mosts is lighter than nothing," wrote Lady Robertland, who lived dynamically in the seventeenth century, "and without God, the least of leasts is heavier than any burden."

Often tiredness and unhappiness walk hand and hand, and it can be said that vitality and joy have a way of skipping along together. It is a true statement and cannot be said too often — what a person believes is directly connected with how he feels. There *is* joy in believing God. "Being confident of this very thing, that he which hath begun a good work in you will perform it" (Phil. 1:6). What can give you more joy, more energy than knowing that what you are doing now, by the grace of God, will in His timing be exactly what He wants it to be. As Luther said in one of his difficult moments, "Be that as it may, God is God"; and he continued with the confidence and vigor which was the soul of his life, "Man is almost always mistaken in his judgments; but this is our God. He will lead us with goodness for ever and ever."

Foolishly we leave the Bible alone, because we have heard that it is full of errors and myths, not worth troubling over, or we're too busy, or.... As one looks back into history, one cannot help but notice the remarkable vitality of such men as Moses, David, Paul, Mark, Luther, Spurgeon, Meyer, Moody, to mention only a few of God's great, energetic men.

The Bible is full of articulate and reasoned statements of eternal truth that the deepest and most sensitive minds in each age have found to be utterly reliable and timely and infinitely worth knowing. The majestic words speak from generation to generation, from heart to heart. Are we going to let the tired, run-down, unenlightened men of this age turn us away from the one thing that can cause us to "mount up with wings as eagles"?

"Every purpose of the Lord shall be performed," says the Word of God (Jer. 51:29). Is this not an encouragement to go on in faith today? "But how?" we sigh, when we are weary and spent. Isaiah presents a triumphant, realistic and practical answer which will put a lilt and a spark in our tired bones:

"He giveth power to the faint; and to them that have no might he increaseth strength. Even the youths shall faint and be weary, and the young men shall utterly fall: But they that wait upon the Lord shall renew their strength; they shall mount up with wings as eagles; they shall run, and not be weary; and they shall walk, and not faint" (Isa. 40:29-31).

24. Better Than Nothing

It is difficult to be happy with little in life, but even harder with a lot. "Never have so many had it so good," said a banker in New York city, "and been so miserable about it all."

I correspond with a missionary who works among orphans in Formosa. Many of the boys are from the streets where they have been sleeping under boxes and boards, making a living begging, doing odd jobs, and sometimes, stealing. They come into the Christian home ragged and filthy with no concern about their appearance. In their new home they are given a sense of belonging, a place where they can be useful, baths, clean clothes, and even shirts and shoes to wear on Sundays.

My friend, who is busy in the hospital on Sundays, learned from a neighbor that the boys, after they leave church, carefully remove their shoes and shirts and carry them home. As she commented, "They have never had such precious possessions." It was said nearly two thousand years ago that if what you have seems insufficient to you, then, though you possess the world, you will yet be miserable.

Though it is years ago now, I can remember an incident at a camp where I was a counselor one summer. The cook forgot to order hot dogs for a cook-out, and at the last minute a few sandwiches left over from the day before were substituted. It was a skimpy meal for twenty-six active, young girls who had just been on a five-mile hike; but the cook had other things on her mind and was not in the mood to discuss the situation.

The head counselor of our group was furious, but saved her complaints for the staff meeting the following day. To the hungry campers standing in line she tactfully explained that there had been a mix-up in the kitchen and we would all have to make the best of it. Of course, a few grumbled, but the majority took it well, and one small child, when handed her stale sandwich and plum, shrugged her shoulders and grinned, "It's better than nothing!"

It is as the apostle Paul told the Philippians, a satisfying way to live: "I have learned, in whatever state I am, therewith to be content" (Phil. 4:11).

25. A Different Angle

There is excitement in our end of town. Some neighbors are moving to Borneo. The only trouble, the wife isn't excited. Quite the contrary, she's dreading it. "We've been talking about it for months," she explained, "but last night when Bill came home and told me he had actually been accepted, everything inside me revolted. I can't imagine myself or the children adjusting to such a different life; but at the same time I felt dreadful, because Bill is genuinely enthusiastic about going. What can I do?" She added quickly, "Don't tell me to pray, please! That's all I've been doing for fifteen hours." Then she smiled weakly, "Well, maybe all of it wasn't prayer; part of it plain worry and anxiety!"

The only time I offer "advice" to friends is when it is asked for, and, believe me, even then, it is well to proceed cautiously. We all walk in different shoes.

The idea is this — if you have something hard ahead of you, something you'd *really* rather not do, but have to do, approach it from a different angle. One of the best approaches to a difficult situation is to think of the impending hardship as an opportunity. An opportunity to... well, if you can't think of anything else, an opportunity to develop patience. Which one of has learned all we need to know about *that*. Quite often you come upon in the Psalms, "How long, Lord?" It is an ancient, thorny problem, learning to be patient. It could easily be worth a trip to Borneo to be able to return as a grounded and settled Christian.

In talking over the problems of the missionary's wife we both agreed she had to free her mind of the negative thoughts about Borneo that were swarming about her head like a flock of starlings. Instead she had to focus her attention on the fact that what she and her family were being offered was actually a privilege. We were not stretching a point. Not everyone gets to make a trip around the world, meet new people with different backgrounds, and see and do things that those who stay home can never experience.

And next she would have to make up her mind from the beginning not to be forever saying, "In the U.S.A. we do so-and-so," and so-and-so. Study about the country to which you are going, to be observant, and learn from the differences; which does not mean you have to *like* everything, nor will you be able completely to eradicate such thoughts as, there is *nothing* to equal American plumbing, American hamburgers, American efficiency, American cheerfulness and American gas stations, motels, supermarkets, and ice in water.

Then we reminisced about when she and her husband first moved to Chicago. It had seemed far from Nebraska, and strange, but after they had made friends, joined a church and began living useful, busy lives, it became home. The fact that they had found congenial people in Chicago should be an encouragement that they will make friends in Borneo, too. Then, also, as soon as they discover that they are needed in Borneo, which they surely will be, if they want to be, their lives will take on significance. One secret in living is, keep busy, keep happy.

Finally, we talked about the importance of the "light" touch. It rarely harms a difficult situation to laugh a little. It is often the one thing needed. When two people marry, it is "for better or worse." A complaining wife can make of marriage something, not only "worse," but the very worst, if she does not live according to the precept: "By the grace of God, I will stand by my husband, faithfully, cheerfully and bravely, even if he decides to go to ... Borneo!"

Before she left, we read Matthew 28, which ends on this thought: "And mind you, I am alongside you all the days until the end of the age. Amen." (*Berkeley Version*) We decided that must mean Borneo, too.

26. Are Schools Necessary?

The other day a leading anthropologist suggested that we might be better off if we did away with schools. I got this from a newspaper article I was reading. In my own weak-brained musings I, too, have felt there must be a solution to the educational problem that leans toward saving money, not always spending more. As I observe my older friends and relatives who were educated in the "little, red schoolhouse," I can't grasp what they've missed by not attending a five-million dollar school with an all white roof.

What sort of musical training did they get? — ask the progressives. It wasn't much, I guess, but all my aunts play the piano and sing and remember with enthusiasm a wide variety of songs and hymns they have known since childhood. *Well, that might be, but they surely were lacking in the fundamentals.* I've noticed that if my nieces and nephews want to spell a word correctly, they always ask Grandma, or if they've forgotten the main capitals of the world, she refreshes their minds. Then I recall an incident when my mother was balancing her checkbook. She looked at my father who was reading the newspaper, and said quietly, "It doesn't balance. The bank must have made an error."

My father was greatly amused (those were the days bank didn't make mistakes), but he laughed harder the day mother received a notice from the bank acknowledging they had made an error.

Well, in the old schools they certainly were weak in art and science. Several of the "little red schoolhouse" graduates have lovely dishes they have painted themselves. Others have made, and continue to make, braided rugs, hand-embroidered cloths, quilts, bedspreads, real collectors' items; and the only time I received "A" in biology was when I borrowed a butterfly collection made by an older relative.

Yes, but they did not have the variety of entertainment that we give the children today. That's true. It still takes little to make them happy. I have seen my mother hold a roomful of children spellbound with a piece of paper and pencil, or some string and buttons, foolish games she learned in the country school....

To continue with the plan of the anthropologist: Her theory is that schools are a necessity in a society which wishes to become literate in one generation, but today nearly everyone in the U.S.A. can read. And so to solve the serious financial problem, she proposes that mothers rather than schools teach their children to read.

At first glance, this cannot help but strike the taxpayer as a superb idea, but I hasten to add, as a friend of many mothers, the anthropologist has overlooked a point. I'm not trained in these matters, of course, and this is only my opinion, but frequent visits with families where there are many children has convinced me that schools are for the sake of parents, not children.

Anyone who has been in a home where there are six children, and five of them are absent from school with the mumps, knows what I am talking about. In the midst of such liveliness stands one wild-eyed mother, who with her bare fists, will build the first school in the new social order if the anthropologist is successful in doing away with schools!

The important thing, it would seem to me, whether we have large, expensive schools, small schools, or no schools, is that the children gain wisdom, the wisdom which comes from above. "For wisdom is better than rubies," according to the best authority we have, the Scriptures, "and all the things that may be desired are not to be compared to it" (Prov. 8:11).

27. Not Trying

A prominent professor, who is also a minister, said in an interview, "I am not trying to convert anyone." He explained that his classes are "an appeal to reason," and their purpose is "to introduce students to the complexities of religion-life involvement."

More recently the teacher and clergyman has appeared on a nation-wide TV program, and it is safe to conclude that none of his viewers have been converted either. It makes me want to ask questions.

What has happened to the leaders of the Christian church? Are they ashamed of the gospel of Jesus Christ? Do they think that there are several ways to God and that the Lord was making small talk when He said: "I am the way, the truth and the life: No man comes unto the Father, but by me" (John 14:6)?

Has it ceased to be true that Christ is able to save to the uttermost those who come to God by Him? Is modern man so adjusted, so happy, so sound, so peaceful that these words no longer mean anything to him: "My peace I give unto you: not as the world giveth, give I unto you. Let not your heart be troubled, neither let it be afraid" (John 14:27)?

There are hundreds and thousands of people (myself included) who shall be everlastingly thankful that the Francis Schaeffer family of L'Abri Fellowship and their many helpers do not limit themselves to discussions about the complexities of religion-life involvement. (What modern man is not aware of complexities, the opening and shutting of a thousand doors that lead nowhere?) No, we needed to hear about the God of the impossible who is sovereign, holy, righteous, and how He gave the treasure of His heart, His Son, for us, and what this can mean in our lives when we believe in the Saviour.

Even as I am writing this chapter, a young German student came to the door to thank the singer for her part in helping him to have confidence in the finished work of Christ. He said that this was the first time in his life that he felt settled. Had those at L'Abri only appealed to his reason, he would have returned to his university as mixed-up as ever. In contrast to the minister-professor who is "not trying to convert anyone," all of us in the L'Abri community were praying for Karl the week he was here, that he would be converted. We prayed that he, too, might know the joy of coming into a living relationship with God through faith in Jesus Christ. If you know the best there is, surely you are going to spend the rest of your life telling others.

Can you imagine Martin Luther (also a pastor-professor) not trying to convert his students?

Those who love the Lord are constrained to confess him before men. As McCheyne said, "A lively Christian cannot keep silence."

You can test the rightness of a system by results. Has anyone been converted in your church recently? The world can yet be turned upside down if we would get about the Lord's business of telling others what God has done for us.

28. Not Deep Enough

It is fascinating and fearful to sit in our living rooms and watch history being made. As a niece commented (she was lying on the floor reading the newspaper, doing her homework and watching TV), "I think the whole world's gone crazy!"

Particularly if we approach life without the knowledge which God has revealed about it, it would seem so. The news media has contributed to our confusion and anguish by making certain we haven't missed one scrap of bad news which has taken place in the universe. It is enough for the average human nervous system not to break under the pressures within his own community and family, let alone to try to live cheerfully under the weight of the burdens of the whole world.

Many of us have been praying for revival and reformation in our lands. It is possible we could help hasten the day if we would begin each morning with the encouragement and strength which comes from reading the Scriptures, rather than facing the dawn with loud commercials, unspeakable music, and the usual bad news.

Perhaps we should be thankful we have not been called upon to solve the problems of the world. How do you arrive at rational solutions when often dealing with irrationality? And let's not forget, not one of us can be trusted in our judgment all the way. This should help us to be more sympathetic with one another. It is as Calvin said, "There is no person who is not enveloped with some cloud of ignorance." Now that I have had many years to walk around, I find I'm not as hard on others as I used to be. If you'll notice, young people, politicians and many commentators dwell in the world of "accusing and excusing." The only way to break out of that mold is to recall Christ's way, "When he was reviled, reviled not again: when he suffered, he threatened not: but committed himself to him that judgeth righteously" (I Peter 2:23).

In discussing the problems of a former neighbor, another neighbor said, "The only way out of her trouble, as far as I can see, Lois should never have married Pete!"

That sounds funny, but many who are helping to shape our world have the same lack of logic. They fail to recognize that you have to deal with problems as they are, not as you think they ought to be, or wish they might be. Lois and Peter are married, and their unhappiness will never be resolved by saying they ought not to have married! The solution to their problems, your problems and mine, all the problems in the whole world, must come out of the cold, hard facts as they are. Frankly, I know no other way to soften stubborn reality than to expose the people and their problems to the love of God — not man's idea of the love of God, but the authentic love of God which will not let go. Human love does not penetrate deep enough into tangled, twisted situations with a history of "accusing and excusing." Where there has been trouble, bad trouble, as the hymn writer has said it, "In times like these, you need a Saviour."

A young couple I know, recently decided to get a divorce. Their situation was going from bad to worse. There seemed no point in going on together. But before making it official, to satisfy a friend whom they both respected, they went to see her pastor.

They had a long, straight talk concerning man's obligation to God, and what God will do for man if he will listen and obey. As a parting remark, the minister said, "I ask one thing of you. Wait a week before you go to your lawyer, and in this time read I Corinthians 13 every day, and ask God to help you understand the words; then every night pray aloud together."

It is curious what happens in the heart when you hear the

person who has been giving you a bad time pray in your presence, "Lord, forgive me, I've been so selfish. O God, help me to be a better husband." It makes you want to be less selfish yourself. But I must say, it is hard on the legal profession. The young couple never went to the lawyer.

The human spectacle when seen in the light of the revelation of Jesus Christ is bright with hope. The press and TV are making sure we know the bad news of today; we Christians have the privilege of telling the world the good news. "This is his commandment, That we should believe on the name of his Son Jesus Christ, and love one another, as he gave us commandment. And he that keepeth his commandments dwelleth in him, and he in him. And hereby we know that he abideth in us, by the Spirit which he hath given us" (I John 3:23, 24).

29. Not Always Doing

While leafing through a magazine in the waiting room of a dentist I saw a cartoon which showed a man and a woman at a counter marked, "Educational Toys." A clerk was showing them a box filled with odd-shaped pieces. "These fragments," he said, "are designed to prepare children for today's complex world. No matter how they are put together, it doesn't come out right."

But it is not only in the twentieth century that things do not always come out right, nor do we see the final solutions to all things in our lifetime. This has been going on for a long, long time. There is always a bothersome, "But..." in life, or an irksome, "If...," and we must not leave out the disenchanting, "However...."

Who doesn't know a fine young lawyer, or a hard-working fireman, or a brilliant professor, but..., and any number of painful flaws can be supplied. "He is the grandest person, *but* he drinks too much." Or, when was the last time you heard: "Jim is the nicest fellow, *but* he has a dreadful temper." "Yes sir, she is the loveliest lady, *but*..., and it goes on and on.

Then all of us live part of our lives in the dismal shade of, "IF.... If I didn't have financial worries, I'd be a great artist. If my back (head, tooth, or right toe) would stop aching, I'd mow the lawn or wash the dishes. If I were married, I'd be on the mission field. If it wasn't for that old barn, we'd have the best view in the world. If I had the breaks of my brother-in-law, I'd... IF... IF...IF....

And "However..." is nearly the peskiest of all. The enthusiasm-squelchers dote on, "However...." Here is an example:

You have just presented to the board a wonderful idea how the Sunday School could be better organized. You have spent weeks working out the plan, and have through your enthusiasm caused nearly all of the teachers to agree to the change. And so at the meeting when the new plan comes up for the vote, a member, who hasn't been to a meeting in six months, and has no practical experience in teaching, drops one neat, "However...." and wins over all those who can't stand change. When the vote is taken, the wonderful idea loses, six to five.

A learned Frenchman said, "We cannot always be doing a great work, but we can always be doing something that belongs to our condition. To be silent, to suffer, to pray when we cannot act, is acceptable to God."

As we go on in life, it becomes clearer and clearer that things do not always work out as we see them in our mind. In this world which sin has tainted, kindness is sometimes rebuffed, goodness seems to go unnoticed, faithfulness, apparently unrewarded, and love often abused; but we learn from the One who suffered and died for us, that to serve and love Him is its own reward, no matter, "If... But... or However...."

"The Lord is my strength and my shield; my heart trusted in him, and I am helped; therefore my heart greatly rejoiceth; and with my song will I praise him.... I will joy in the God of my salvation" (Ps. 28:7 and Hab. 3:18).

30. A Few Friends at the End

Once in a while you read something that is meant for you, that you wish you could memorize, or next best that you can tape to a cupboard door and glance at in moments of need. Maybe it will say something to you, too. As different as we are, in some respects many of us are uncomfortably alike.

Here are the words of wisdom. I do not know who wrote it, but I do say, thank you, anyway:

"Lord, Thou knowest better than I know myself that I am growing older and will someday be old. Keep me from getting talkative, and particularly, from the fatal habit of thinking I must say something on *every* subject.

"Release me from craving to try to straighten out everybody's affairs. Make me thoughtful, but not moody; helpful, but not bossy. With my 'vast store of wisdom,' it seems a pity not to use all of it — but Thou knowest, Lord, that I want a few friends at the end.

"Keep my mind free from the recital of endless details; give me wings to get to the point! Seal my lips on my aches and pains — they are increasing and my love of rehearsing them is becoming sweeter as the years go by. Teach me the glorious lesson that occasionally it is possible that even I may be mistaken." — Author unknown

It is as it says in Scripture, "A merry heart doeth good like a medicine; but a broken spirit drieth the bones" (Prov. 17:22).

Postlude

Make a joyful noise unto the
 Lord, all ye lands.
Serve the Lord with gladness:
 come before his presence with singing.
Know ye that the Lord he is God:
 it is he that hath made us,
and not we ourselves: we are his
 people, and the sheep of his pasture.
Enter into his gates with thanksgiving,
 and into his courts with praise:
be thankful unto him,
 and bless his name.
For the Lord is good; his mercy
 is everlasting; and his truth
endureth to all generations.

       Psalm 100